LAND FOR PEOPLE

LAND TENURE AND THE VERY POOR

by

Claire Whittemore

OXFAM PUBLIC AFFAIRS UNIT

First published in 1981

© Oxfam 1981

ISBN 0 85598 046 X

Printed by Henry Stone & Son (Printers) Ltd.,
Banbury, Oxon.

Published by Oxfam, 274 Banbury Road,
Oxford OX2 7DZ

Contents

Foreword

The purpose of this report is to consider the question of land ownership in the Third World in the light of Oxfam's overseas programme of rural development. It is thus different from more scholarly studies. It describes Oxfam's increasing awareness of the difficulties and pitfalls related to land tenure and power structures — problems which have to be overcome by the rural people Oxfam supports if they are even to begin to escape from their poverty. It also examines the policies and activities of international, governmental, aid and investment institutions and asks whether they are really helping the poorest of the poor or, in fact, further impoverishing them.

The views expressed in this report result from a wide-ranging series of discussions with Oxfam staff and consultants, both overseas and in Britain.

It is hoped that journalists, students and writers will use the report as a stimulus to research more deeply into the questions raised. It is also hoped that people who work or are interested in the 'development' field will find it a useful contribution to the continuing debate on the eradication of poverty.

Abbreviations

1. BRAC   Bangladesh Rural Advancement Committee
2. FAO   Food and Agriculture Organisation
3. FCI   Food Corporation of India
4. FFW   Food-for-work
5. GNP   Gross national product
6. HYV   High yield variety
7. IBRD   International Bank for Reconstruction and Development
8. IDA   International Development Association
9. ILO   International Labour Organisation
10. NGO   Non-governmental organisation
11. PL480   Public Law 480 (United States of America)
12. UN   United Nations
13. UNCTAD   United Nations Conference on Trade and Development
14. UNRISD   United Nations Research Institute for Social Development
15. US   United States
16. USA   United States of America
17. WCARRD   World Conference on Agrarian Reform and Rural Development

 **Introduction**

1.   Unjust land tenure systems and the political, economic and social policies which enable these systems to prevail are the chief causes of hunger and poverty in the Third World today.

2.   If a rural family or community has secure use of a piece of land, they will almost certainly grow their own food before they consider any other crops. The same land in the hands of a landlord, a government, or a foreign firm, is far more likely to be used to grow whatever is most profitable, which probably would not be food for local consumption.

3.   Land ownership in the Third World is very highly concentrated. For example, in South America in 1973, the top 2% of the farming population controlled 47% of the land.[1] In India, the top 22% of the landowners hold 76% of the land — a figure almost unchanged for 20 years.[2] So the majority of rural people do not have control over the land resources in the areas where they live.

4.   Nearly three quarters of all the people on earth make some kind of living by cultivating the land. From their ranks come the vast majority of the world's estimated 800 million living in extreme poverty and hunger.[3] Millions more are on the brink.

5.   This report is an attempt to explain why Oxfam considers rural poverty in much of the Third World to be not merely a technical problem — a consequence of too little food, or lack of agricultural development — but rather a complex social, economic and political problem, with the control and ownership of land central to the whole issue. It also raises the question of whether much of the international, intergovernmental aid to the agricultural sector only reinforces the power structures which keep the poorest rural people as they are. In order to explain Oxfam's present stance, it is necessary to look back a few years.

6.   At the 1974 World Food Conference both the national delegations and the multilateral aid agencies placed a great deal of emphasis on the need to produce more food throughout the world. The implication was that there was a race between population growth and increased agricultural production. The discussions tended to treat food production and food distri-

bution as two distinct problems which could be dealt with separately. The solutions proposed were technical and economic.

7. The majority of the NGOs and academics present at the Conference challenged the official view that the problem was one of food scarcity. They argued that there was already enough food in the world for everyone, but that millions of people still went hungry because world food supplies were maldistributed. They denounced the way in which food industries used up basic food-stuffs, especially grains, to produce high-value foods for the rich world. They pointed to the fact that, through eating grain-fed meat, people in rich countries consume about five times more grain than those in developing countries. Oxfam, along with many other similar agencies, argued for a fairer distribution of world grain supplies.

8. Not many of the delegates or lobbyists took full acount of the political and social barriers which keep people hungry. Only a handful of people were talking in such terms at that time.

9. During the six years since the World Food Conference, a very lively debate has been in progress between NGOs, academics and activists on the food and hunger question. The participants in the debate have split into two main groups.

10. One group still takes the view that was propounded by most NGOs at the World Food Conference. They still argue that a better distribution of the food available in the world should be the goal. To achieve this they suggest that nations in the Third World should be helped through aid and trade concessions to increase employment and thus improve their buying power. They, therefore, try to influence and improve the outcome of international conferences such as UNCTAD, and the discussions on a possible New International Economic Order. Many members of this group also use the self-interest argument: they urge governments of rich countries to see that it is in their own interests to make these international changes, because the result would be the opening up of new markets for the rich countries.

11. The view of the second group can be divided into three main arguments.

    a) They accept that it may be necessary to press for change in the international terms of trade, given the present world system of production and trade. They argue, however, that this view does not take into account the fact that many developing country governments and wealthy elites will not pass on these new trading benefits to the poor people who form the vast majority of the rural Third World population. They believe that the inequalities of power, wealth and particularly of land distribution need to be reduced first. They argue that local and national food self-reliance should be a priority in any country's development.

b) They consider that much of the official aid and investment which supposedly help the rural poor are doing them more harm than good through supporting the very mechanisms which perpetuate poverty. The aid which they see as really useful involves very small scale programmes which support rural people's own efforts to change their lives.

c) They consider that private investment in the agricultural sector of developing countries is rarely in the interests of the poor. It does not provide them with more employment and it uses land to grow crops which the poor cannot afford to buy. They are especially concerned about the activities of the major multinational companies, which are particularly difficult to control.

12. There is truth in the arguments of both these groups but, on balance, Oxfam increasingly finds itself allied with the latter rather than the former. The issues raised in this report have emerged from the process of Oxfam constantly reviewing and questioning its own policies.

13. Oxfam has evolved in the last thirty years from a disaster relief organisation into one which also puts strong emphasis on long-term development. It has been a process which has caused much internal examination. During the sixties long-term development was viewed by Oxfam as a matter of providing technical equipment and technical educational support. In the agricultural sector, we provided such items as tractors and agricultural training to small farmers' groups. Increasingly, however, Oxfam Field Staff in the Third World reported that local and national power structures and the associated systems of land tenure and methods of controlling credit and marketing were major inhibiting factors in creating, promoting and funding agricultural development programmes which really reach the very poor peasants. (This is illustrated in Chapter 2.)

14. One consequence of this increasing awareness of the power structures related to landholding is that Oxfam has had to admit that many of its past agricultural projects were built on shaky foundations, because the tenure the poor had on the land was not secure. A landlord or government could have chosen at any time to evict the people from the land where Oxfam had funded technical advances. Now, one of the very important priorities of the locally based Field Staff is to check on the land tenure position, before any agricultural project can be considered for funding.

15. Thus, Oxfam's approach to rural development has shifted from simply providing technical aid to putting more emphasis on social development: helping poor rural people to build up an awareness of those parts of the system which take advantage of them. Several projects are now funded which give legal advice about land problems, under existing legislation; projects which help people to obtain credit at reasonable rates of interest; projects which help them form marketing cooperatives in order to try to prevent the profits of their labour going to speculators. Oxfam has long been concerned with another aspect of land tenure — the fact that it is very difficult to aid people who have no land and who are dependent on seasonal agricultural work. In the past Oxfam has attempted to help them by providing alternative work but now it is also supporting their efforts to claim fairer wages for their seasonal labour.

16. Chapter 2 discusses, in the light of Oxfam's experience, land tenure and the accompanying political and social problems which keep rural people poor. In Chapter 3 the issues of land reform, food self-reliance and the structures which inhibit these are discussed. In both these Chapters the report concentrates mainly on Asia and Latin America because the same land and power related problems in Africa have not emerged as prominently in Oxfam's project experience. However, the way in which land and wealth are now being increasingly concentrated into fewer hands in parts of Africa *is* recognised and described.

17. In the process of reviewing and questioning policies, Oxfam Field Staff and advisers also commented on the role of multilateral and bilateral aid and investment agencies whose development programmes are aimed mostly at overall economic growth, which is a very different aim from that of reducing poverty or aiding the poorest. Therefore, the benefit to the poorest of the poor of this type of aid was questioned. Several of the Field Directors reported their concern that the benefits of many official aid projects were supporting the middle strata of rural society, sometimes at the expense of the poor, and were actually reinforcing the structures which perpetuate poverty. So it is then pertinent to ask what are the consequences of this aid on the poorest of the rural poor? Is official aid and investment often positively harmful to the very poor?

18. Chapter 4 looks at the way multilateral aid and investment agencies work in the rural sector and gives some examples of the sort of aid policies and activities that are being questioned. The report also considers how the development theories of these agencies and governments were presented and challenged in Rome in July 1979 at World Conference on Agrarian Reform and Rural Development (WCARRD), held by the FAO.

2 Why the Rural Poor Stay Poor

19.   Tenant farmers, sharecroppers and landless labourers form the vast mass of poor men, women and children who work on the land. They work long and strenuous hours but they are seldom able to get a fair return for their labour or to choose freely what they grow, eat, sell or buy. They have little or no control over the production or distribution of food. They stay poor because the land and their lives are controlled by systems which usually favour the rich and at best ignore the poor. This Chapter describes the aims of groups of rural people with whom Oxfam has worked and the way in which their efforts have often been thwarted and oppressed by these systems. The reader will find some of the project descriptions tantalisingly brief but it is necessary to protect the people whose efforts are supported by Oxfam.

Land and Power in Rural Latin America

20.   Latin America is the most striking case of marked inequalities in the distribution of power and wealth. Tenants and sharecroppers survive on small plots of their landlord's land while landless labourers are dependent on finding seasonal work from the big landowners. A small number of landlords and employers own the majority of the agricultural land. A good illustration of this is Brazil.

Distribution and Area of Farms in Brazil in 1972*

	Number	%	Area (hectares)	%
Smallholdings	2,437,001	72	46,277,000	12
Agricultural enterprises	162,802	5	35,967,000	10
Large estates	787,370	23	288,026,000	78
	3,387,173	**100**	**370,270,000**	**100**

* The landless (seasonal and day labourers), who outnumber smallholders, are not included in these figures. Their numbers increase every year as the rural population loses its access to land. The majority are forced to migrate to the cities.

<u>Source</u>: Brazil, Ministry of Agriculture, INCRA, 1972

5

21. As a result of the inequitable distribution of land in Latin America, the vast majority of the population is poor and malnourished. Guatemala, for example, has an infant mortality rate of 83 for every 1000 live births. In parts of the Dominican Republic, this rate can rise as high as 130 per 1000 live births. In Haiti, of children aged up to 6 years, a recent survey showed that only 13% were not suffering malnutrition. [5]

22. A characteristic of rural society in Latin America from the Spanish and Portuguese colonial period until the late 19th century has been the concentration of power in the hands of a small minority. Traditionally, this power group consisted of large estate owners who needed labour on their estates. Very often they provided small plots for tenants who, in return, worked certain days of the week on their landlord's estate. In this way the tenants provided a cheap source of labour. Alternatively, sharecroppers worked pieces of land and gave a share of the crop to the landlord. In many cases these tenants remained in a state of dependence and submission. The power of landlords was legitimised by the Roman Catholic Church which, during the colonial period, was itself a vast landholder. This traditional pattern of landholding remained more or less unchanged about a century ago.

23. In the last hundred years, significant changes have taken place throughout most of Latin America. In the late 19th and early 20th centuries the Church lost much of its land and, more recently, some clergy have emerged who identify very closely with the rural and urban poor. In Mexico, Bolivia and Cuba there has been major reform associated with social revolution. In Argentina, alternatively, a large middle class of 'homestead' farmers emerged towards the end of the 1800s. All these changes could be said to have benefited the majority of the people in the countries concerned.

24. However, for the vast majority of the Latin American countries the changes which have taken place during the present century have reinforced the pattern of inequality in wealth, income and power which emerged in Latin America during the Spanish and Portuguese colonial empires. Today, the traditional landlord/tenant relationship still continues unchanged in some areas and countries; in others, such as Brazil, Central America and Colombia, the development of urban industries, requiring raw materials such as cotton, encouraged landlords to evict the tenants and sharecroppers from their estates to make way for large-scale commercial crop production. These landowners now only require a seasonal labour force for harvesting the produce since other operations are often mechanised. In the past, the majority of people had some access to the land and could produce for themselves as well as for their landlord; now a large proportion of them are landless and dependent on what work they

can find, either rural or urban. In recent years there has been a heavy migration to the towns by landless people in search of work. About half the people of Latin America now live in towns and cities and mostly they suffer a level of poverty little different from their rural counterparts.

25. In the rural areas the remaining peasantry have very varied access to land. Many are now landless labourers looking for seasonal paid work and most of the rest are still tenants on large estates. A few have obtained legal title to the land they farm through some type of land reform. This can be a mixed blessing.

26. Those peasants with some access to land as tenants or even as small owners are today incorporated into new power structures because landowning elites have tended to move to towns in recent years and have diversified their economic interests into commerce and industry. The landowners have build up close links with the military and their political allies. The seat of power has thus shifted from the rural to the urban areas, so what happens in the urban economy now affects the rural economy.

27. The landowner is able, directly or indirectly, to influence the new power structures. The civil servant or economist in the Ministry of Agriculture, the manager of the local branch of the agricultural credit bank, the property company, the merchant who fixes prices, the lorry owner who transports crops to market, are all, in a way, acting on behalf of the landowner. For instance, the bank system in Colombia is such that although the small peasant deposits his money there, the lending policies are all directed to large scale farming. The means by which the power of the landowning group is maintained is now more varied, although direct oppression of tenants is still very common.

28. In the past, peasant families subsisted on the land they tenanted. Now, however, most of them have been drawn into the market economy in one way or another. For instance, they are more likely to be required to pay rent in cash than through labour or a percentage of their crops, so they must market part of their crop to earn cash. Now, not only do they have problems in controlling agricultural production, but also they have to worry about their lack of control of distribution and marketing. So even landowning peasants are not necessarily better off if they still live in an unequal power system.

29. Oxfam is working with a wide variety of groups within the rural economy. Support work includes helping landless labourers to organise, supporting dispossessed squatters and tenants in their struggle to secure their rights under the law, funding groups who are trying to form credit unions, as well as helping with general agricultural aid.

Lack of Security

30. A serious difficulty faced by many tenant farmers is a lack of security of tenure. Although many countries have legislation requiring all contracts to be written and to have legal status, a high proportion of tenancy agreements are verbal, which is to the advantage of the landlord should he wish to evict his tenants.

31. This lack of security acts as a major disincentive to improving land. In south-west Haiti, for instance, a man using traditional methods on good land would barely break even. With techniques taught by an Oxfam-supported project, he could make £120 net profit annually on the average size holding (1.4 hectares). But people on rented land are reluctant to make improvements, especially long term ones such as contour-terracing or soil-improvement, because if they do the landlord is liable to take back the land or put up the rent. One of the teachers on an Oxfam-supported project has twice had his land taken back in this way.[6] In some countries in Latin America (eg Brazil) the law allows for compensation for improvements but a peasant would normally need the assistance of sympathetic lawyers to claim his rights within the rule of law.

Investment in Land

32. A frequent motive for eviction is the rise in land values with 'opening up' of land for highly commercial agriculture. This is occurring on a large scale throughout Latin America and particularly in the interior of Brazil where capital-intensive cattle ranches are displacing the existing peasants, a process involving a high degree of local violence. Often these expanding estates are financed not by individual landowners but by business consortia, in many instances multinational companies primarily interested in the profits of food production for export and in the security of a good investment. Susan George has documented this situation in some detail in her two books. [7] Oxfam Field Staff would support most of the points she makes on Latin America.

Legal Rights

33. Although there are laws in many Latin American countries giving peasants guaranteed rights to the land they work, often they are not enforced. In some cases the landowners hire gunmen to drive out the local peasants. Local police and judges often side with the landowners (or even are the landowners), so the peasants lack protection from the law. Without legal aid peasants can be cheated and evicted easily.

34. There are differences between the laws in the various countries of Latin America but similarities in the ways in which they are abused. There are

two main areas of abuse. Firstly, an estate owner can attempt to evict his tenants because he wants to use the land for other purposes. These tenants have rights in law but are subject to intimidation, unfulfilled promises of compensation and trickery. A second form of legal abuse happens when a small landowner's title is through inheritance or by settlement and there is thus no documented title to the land. Such people are subject to intimidation when spurious title is claimed by commercial interests or large landowners anxious to expand their holdings. In such cases police and political connivance is common.

35.   In 1970, the construction of a new road to open up the Amazon Basin encouraged large-scale cattle ranchers to move into the area. Land was cheap and fertile and occupied by rural day labourers, tenant farmers, sharecroppers and squatters who were responsible for the production of manioc, beans, maize and castor oil plants. A period of violent expulsion without compensation began for the peasants, although the tenants, if not the others, had legal rights. The landlords sold their land for a substantial profit while conversion of cultivated land to pasture for cattle resulted in a scarcity of staple foods and in increases in prices.

36.   A lawyer was recruited to advise the peasant communities and to defend them in court. There were already numerous well-documented cases of violence and the lawyer took several of these to court, where they have been shelved for a considerable period of time. The barrier to justice presented by the combination of powerful interests (judges, the police and landowners) proved impassable. The work of the lawyer and other community workers in the area, as elsewhere, has, therefore, shifted its emphasis to educational work. This involved the lawyer, priests, community workers and representatives in explaining, at courses and meetings, the peasants' rights and encouraging membership of the official rural workers' organisations through which they have a greater chance of obtaining justice and secure access to land. [8]

37.   Another example comes from Nicaragua under General Somoza, where, in the mid 1970s, 90 Indian families were thrown off reserve land in Los Arcos by a wealthy landowner who wanted to extend his cotton-growing operation. The Indians, numbering some 600 in all, were reduced to living on the verge of the road.

38.   The landowner was supported by the National Guard. The peasants sought the help of the Buffette Popular, a legal aid clinic in Leon. Though the land had traditionally been an Indian preserve, no title had been given. However, the aid clinic's lawyers were able to show that the landowner who claimed to have bought the land had no papers to prove his claim either. Over a 5 year period, the Indians managed to recover some 650

acres through the courts. At first, when they tried to reoccupy the land, they suffered harassment from the National Guard who arrested members of the community, beat them up and threw them in gaol.

39. The re-possessed land is now divided three ways: a communal part, the proceeds from which pay for a teacher, medicines, seed, insecticides, etc; another communally-owned part, from which each farmer receives the equivalent of his input (which is timed); and individually-held 3½ acre plots. [9]

Credit and Marketing

40. Very small-scale tenant farmers and owner farmers face severe problems as a result of being drawn into the market economy. The most important people in a peasant farmer's life are the 'middle-men' — the lorry owner, merchant and moneylender, who are often the same person. They are the most visible part of the power structure which ensures that the peasant stays poor. Behind them are the bankers, buyers and mill-owners. Some efforts are being made by locally-organised groups to help peasants to recognise and overcome the limitations which these middle-men enforce on them. Educational programmes have been set up and marketing co-operatives have been formed. One example is a project run by an association of small scale potato farmers in the Cochabamba Valley where the stress is placed on an integrated programme of education, organisation and economic improvement. The realisation is that, while better crop production and cooperative marketing are of some benefit to the farmer, the key to long term improvement lies in an awareness of the problems and in organisation in defence of members' interests. [10]

Landless Labourers

41. Extreme poverty is to be found more often among landless rural labourers (men, women and children) than in any other social group in Latin America. There are several ways in which landless labourers find work. Some live in one area (often squatting on land to which they have no secure legal right) and they work for one large landowner whenever work is seasonally available. Others migrate, according to the seasons, from area to area or even from country to country, finding what agricultural work they can, or they migrate to and from towns, finding a little agricultural work for part of the year and a little industrial work at other times. Many of these people started life as rural workers but have gravitated to the towns looking for work.

42. All these landless labouring groups could, in theory, unite to insist on fair wages and conditions of work, as well as to protect their rights against

arbitrary dismissal without compensation. An example here is an Oxfam-supported programme to assist some of the 70,000 cotton pickers who emigrate from highland Bolivia for the harvest in the Eastern Lowlands. One of the main agents of exploitation is the labour contractor who engages workers in the highlands for the landowners in the east. Attempts are being made, under difficult conditions, to encourage highland communities to cooperate in organising their own work teams, thus eliminating the middle-man. [11] But the resistance of the landowners and employers, combined with the high mobility of labourers, who typically move from a harvest in one area to a harvest in another, makes it difficult to achieve a stable organisation. Workers on plantations find it easier to organise, though they too are vulnerable to repression by the interest groups who see them as a threat.

Land and Power in Rural Asia

43. Land tenure in Asia has developed in very diverse ways. There is, however, one common feature — a hierarchy of landlords with each dominating the next level of sub-tenant. This system ensures that the poor stay poor.

44. While power structures remain as they are, it is very difficult for any real improvements to be made in the lives of rural people in Asia, either through their own efforts or with outside support. In the next few pages, this report attempts to explain the sort of problems that peasants in Asia face and some of the efforts they have made to solve them, sometimes with Oxfam's support. All these issues are closely interlinked, but for convenience they are examined separately.

Security of Tenure

45. Throughout Asia, security of tenure is a major problem. For instance, in India the land of the 40 million Adivasi (the original inhabitants of India) is safeguarded by law against expropriation by outsiders. However, the continuing appropriation of Adivasi land by traders, moneylenders and merchants from outside is widespread. The Adivasis are easily tricked into signing or mortgaging away their land. Several Oxfam-assisted projects in Gujarat and Madhya Pradesh have taken up land cases and instances of exploitation and harassment, which the Adivasis themselves could neither afford nor dare to do. They have been successful in getting land returned and that success has had the effect of warning some of those who thought the Adivasis easy prey. This is expensive and tedious work. In a typical case in Madhya Pradesh a worker, acting for some Adivasi farmers dispossessed of their land, had to journey for months between the village where the land in dispute was situated, his own office in another village, the Forest Officer in a town 30 miles away, a lawyer in a large town 100

miles away, the Collector (District Magistrate) in a town 100 miles the other way, and Government officials in the capital of the State several hundred miles away. There was no telephone and the farmers were illiterate, so he had to keep in constant personal touch with them all. This is an example of the sort of project which Oxfam supports which needs very little financial input but a lot of very committed support from the people working on it. [12]

Landless Labourers

46.   With the introduction of some modernisation and mechanisation of agriculture in Asia, landowners are buying up more land and using less labour and the number of landless peasants is increasing. It is particularly difficult to help and support landless people because there are so many political and social factors working against them. Below are descriptions of three projects where Oxfam has tried to help landless people.

Loans for the Landless

47.   One Oxfam-funded project which directly assists the landless is an agricultural cooperative near Aricha in Bangladesh. In December 1977, Oxfam approved a grant of £5,150 which was placed as a fixed deposit with a bank against a loan for this sum to poor and marginal farmers. Local landowners lent 30 acres of land on a five year lease to 50 landless peasants. They cultivated High Yield Variety (HYV) rice together with three acres of HYV wheat. Unfortunately, early and heavy rains damaged one quarter of the total paddy, thus reducing the yield. Even so, the project was able to repay the bank the first year's loan although the profit for the farmer was much less than anticipated. At present, 80 previously landless peasants are cultivating 53 acres of land on which they expect to grow two crops per year.

48.   In 1978, the Government proclaimed a guaranteed tenure of three years for tenant farmers in an attempt to help the poor and marginal. This is having the opposite effect from that intended: it is deterring landowners from renting out to the same tenants for three years for fear that the land will be turned over to the farmers completely. The cooperative is now running into serious difficulties because the landowners want their land back. [13]

Employment for the Landless

49.   There are not enough programmes in Asia which are designed to encourage landless people to stay and find work in the rural areas rather than to drift to the towns where unemployment, under-employment and low pay are

the norm. It is important that rural employment should support the agriculture of the area through providing implements and services needed by small farmers. Peasant farmers have many needs for service industries and mostly they are dependent on urban markets for goods and services. For illiterate farmers, unfamiliar with towns, prices or technology, getting a tool repaired or an electric motor rewired can prove an expensive business. Small industrial workshops set up in villages can ease this problem. Oxfam has helped with such a workshop, run by landless village people, in a village in Wardha district, Maharashtra (India). The workshop gives both training and employment to landless villagers and also provides peasant farmers with routine repair and fabrication facilities nearby and at reasonable cost. [14]

50. Another Oxfam-supported project in Andhra Pradesh (India) has identified various opportunities for rural employment for the landless, including rope-making, leather-tanning and keeping buffaloes for the production of clarified butter. [15]

Landless Labourers' Unions

51. In India, a variety of laws has been passed which favour the landless labourer, but implementation lags far behind. The focus of peasant movements is to get implemented what is already on the statute book. A group in Maharashtra has formed an agricultural labourers' trade union to negotiate wage rates with the large farmers, and to attempt to enforce the legal minimum agricultural wages. Where bonded labour is still commonplace, labourers need to understand their rights and to organise themselves in order to obtain them.

Credit

52. The only way that most small cultivators in Asia can finance any improvements to their land and crops or recover from a disaster is to go to a moneylender or to borrow from their landlord. Very often the debts become so large that the man has to sell the land he owns, or bond himself (and sometimes his children) like a slave to his landlord as an unpaid labourer.

53. The provision of alternative sources of adequate and timely credit for agricultural purposes is a major requirement for small farming throughout Asia. In India, official regulations make certain categories of farmers (eg Adivasis and Untouchables) and people with incomes of less than £120 a year eligible for loans at preferential rates. There are widespread complaints that because of bureaucracy, the need for repeated visits to Government offices, corruption, etc, the people who most need loans

do not get them, or get less than they need. Often the costs incurred in making an application for a loan far outweigh the value of the loan. A frequent criticism is that loans are not paid out at the right point in the agricultural cycle and are therefore useless.

54.   Oxfam has worked with various commercial banks in different states in India to bridge the gap between the poor farmer and the bank. Oxfam has in some cases put up the security deposit, share capital or collateral against which the bank will make a loan to the small farmers for such items as draught and milk cattle, or seeds and fertiliser.

55.   An example is the long-term agricultural rehabilitation which was needed in several villages in Andhra Pradesh (India) after a cyclone and tidal wave hit them in November, 1977. After desalination of the soil had been completed, the cost of financing the first crop had to be met. Traditionally, the villagers would have gone to moneylenders following a crop failure and they would have had to pay very high rates of interest, possibly as much as 50% per annum. This could lead to bankruptcy and the villager would have had to sell his land or tenancy and become a landless labourer.

56.   The banks were under pressure from the Government to give loans for rehabilitation but very small farmers with less than 2.5 acres of land were considered too high a risk by the banks. Instead of conventionally handing out seed and rice to the villagers, Oxfam decided to deposit money as a security with several banks in Ponnur and Divi Seema, to enable the villagers to borrow money at reasonable interest rates. [16]

Marketing

57.   If the farmer does produce a surplus, he will want to sell it. The power structures which control land and credit often are also involved in marketing, and Oxfam has found great difficulty in helping peasants with marketing (not only in Asia). Some of the same farmers in the credit scheme in Andhra Pradesh (described above) were still, a year later, meeting major problems of marketing.

58.   Over 2,300 small farmers took advantage of the crop loan schemes to buy new seed to plant on land they had struggled to restore after the cyclone. After the rice harvest at the end of 1978, they were advised to sell their produce to the Food Corporation of India (FCI). The FCI price for rice was a minimum of Rs. 63 (£3.83) per bag, while it would only fetch between Rs. 53 (£3.23) and Rs. 57 (£3.47) on the open market. The farmers had to take a sample of their rice for FCI tests and, if it was accepted, they could transport the stock to an FCI store.

59. According to local reports, FCI officials were rejecting most of the samples. This meant the farmers had no alternative but to sell on the open market at a lower price. It was believed locally that the FCI officials collaborated with the merchants who bought the rice after it had been rejected. It was thought that the merchants sold the stock to the FCI later.

60. In cases where rice samples were accepted by the FCI, the small farmer found himself in difficulties again. His stock would only be accepted at the FCI store if it was packed in FCI gunny bags. The farmer had to pay a deposit for the bags at Rs. 5.50 (£0.33) per bag. So he needed money in his pocket before he even sold the rice. Once the stock was delivered he got his deposit back, but finding even a small amount of cash at that time of year was very difficult.

61. According to local post-harvest figures at the beginning of the year there was a surplus of 1.5 million tons of rice in Andhra Pradesh, but the FCI bought only 2,750 tons. [17]

Land and Power in Rural Africa

62. Traditionally, land in Africa was held in common. Communities were self-reliant and developed a high level of social solidarity and egalitarianism. Land was abundant, so the system governing tenure and control of land was based on the need for labour to clear the land in order to bring it under cultivation. The person who cleared the land became the owner and the heirs continued to own the land as a group, each family having the inalienable right to enough land to maintain itself. Thus, group ownership and individual usage of land became the norm.

63. There were certain disruptions to this system, such as attack and conquest by migratory tribal groups, but no major changes took place until the European colonial administrations altered land tenure and usage by creating commercial plantations. For the Europeans, the developing countries represented a vast source of agricultural raw materials. The colonisers destroyed much of the traditional system, and introduced the concept of the market economy in which land and labour were com-modities to be bought and sold. Over the years European domination also had the effect of creating indigenous elites who, for the most part, have continued to promote this type of agricultural development within general development programmes following the western model.

64. The main trend in African agriculture has been towards individualisation of tenure and erosion of traditional group holdings of land, with the exception of such countries as Tanzania. Earnings from export crops have

not benefited the majority of rural people and the disparities between rich and poor are becoming even greater.

65. In this paper, less emphasis has been put on the land tenure problems of Africa than on those of Latin America and Asia. This is simply because the concentration of wealth, land and power into a few hands is in a more advanced state in these continents than in Africa. For this reason, Oxfam Field Staff have experienced far fewer problems related to land in Africa than elsewhere. But unless the trend changes, Africa may well reach the same stage in due course.

66. Zimbabwe and South Africa are both extreme examples of relatively small colonial groups accumulating land and wealth to the detriment of the majority of the people. This has set a trend which will be very difficult for even an independent government to break, since elites are always ready to take over from other elites. In Zimbabwe the whites accumulated approximately the same acreage as the Africans (about 44 million acres) [18] though the Africans formed about 80% of the population. "The land issue provides the focal point around which many of the conflicts of Rhodesian society are centred. Since it is the land structure which plays a fundamental role in the labour supply and wage structure of a colonial society, a structure which has led to increasing numbers of people having to live in poverty." [19]

Control of Food Production and Distribution

67. The control of food production and distribution is a vital issue in Africa, even if it is less obvious than in Asia and Latin America. If the vast majority of the population do not direct either the production or distribution of food, they can go hungry and die of starvation with food still growing in the fields around them, or with full food stores nearby. During the drought and famine of 1972 in the Wollo province of Ethiopia, Oxfam was working in feeding camps where people were dying of starvation. The lorries of the Crown Prince (who was the Governor of Wollo) were passing the camps daily. The lorries contained grain which was going to be sold on the open market. In this case the producer (the Prince) had control of both production and distribution. This was the sort of inhumane and unjust action which contributed to the fall of the Imperial Family in Ethiopia. The people wanted direct access to production and distribution.

Investment in Agriculture

68. Private investment in agriculture can also cause need in an area of plenty. Susan George documents this point well on the Sahel famine, where she describes irrigated ranching in areas where people were starving to death. [20]

In Africa, especially in West Africa, there has been a marked increase in investment in agriculture from western banks and multinational companies. Often these investments reduce the number of people working on the land and crops are frequently sold either as human food or animal feed for western destinations. Since Oxfam does not have direct experience of private investment affecting projects in Africa, no reference has been made to the effects of multinational and other private investment on agriculture there.

3 Land Reform -the Way Forward?

69. The rural poor will be more likely to escape poverty and malnutrition when they obtain some control over food production. A significant number of studies has shown that the productivity per acre is higher when peasants are working on a small-scale labour-intensive basis.[21] They are more likely to achieve this if they have secure use of the land and are not paying large proportions of their crop in rent. Under these conditions they can often produce surpluses for urban use as well as their own needs.

70. To achieve these conditions major structural changes have to take place in many Third World countries. Land is power and no-one gives up power easily.

71. This Chapter looks at various efforts that have been made to reform land tenure. Some could be described as genuine land reforms linked with changes in the power-balance, some as cosmetic changes which keep the balance of power exactly where it was before.

Definitions

72. First, a word on definitions. Definitions are important because people can *imagine* that they are talking about the same thing when, in fact, they are defining crucial terms in different ways. Some people even use these terms specifically because of their ambiguity, in order to conceal their true meaning (which may be more radical or more reactionary than implied). For this reason the terms are defined as they are to be used throughout the rest of this report.

73. *Land reform* means the reform of land tenure systems. Reform can result in either individual, communal or state ownership. Since land and water are usually the basis of power in developing countries, a genuine land reform can only be implemented after there has been a change in power structures, otherwise the 'reform' will only be cosmetic.

74. *Agrarian reform* includes land reform as its most important element but also includes all the necessary institutional reforms which influence or relate to the use of land. Agrarian reform thus includes the introduction of credit and small farmer advice schemes in agricultural techniques and

*1.1 The key to long term improvement lies in an awareness of the problems:
discussions with a field worker at an agricultural cooperative, Zimbabwe.*

1.2 *They work long hours but seldom get a fair return for their labour: transplanting rice, the Philippines.*

1.3 Land reform cannot be done to people: learning to care for coffee seedlings, Haiti.

1.4 Land scarcity is a false obstacle to reform: harvesting paddy, Bangladesh.

marketing, all of which are dependent on the political will to improve the lives of the poor.

Attitudes to Land Reform

75. Reactions to the term 'land reform' are extremely varied. Very few people are actually against reform but, while some see it as the ultimate panacea, others are worried about the likely repercussions and for this reason advise against it.

76. Some people believe that land reform alone can solve the problems of the poor. Because of the importance of land tenure in development and food production, it is easy to conclude that all that has to be done is to achieve a redistribution of the world's land resources as fast as possible by whatever means possible and then poverty and hunger will cease to exist. But land reform is not enough. Even if there was some way of influencing every government in the world to undertake a major reallocation of land, it would be naive to imagine that this would automatically benefit the poor. Land tenure systems are bound up with national power structures and nothing will really change for the poor until these power structures are altered in their favour. To be successful a land reform needs continuing support after it has been implemented. This support has to be political, as well as technical and financial, for the reform to remain successful.

77. Nevertheless, internal and external planners often attempt to alter the systems by financial, technical or legislative means. They try to invent instant land reform packages which can be slotted into any country. They propose international efforts to buy out landlords and they suggest guarantee schemes to take care of change-over periods. Usually the results are disastrous.

78. An example of a reform which can be introduced with good intentions but lead to bad results is tenancy law reform. Strictly speaking, tenancy reform is not land reform as it has been defined above, but it is often treated as such. It is seen as a relatively easy way of improving security of tenure. The result, however, is often quite the reverse. Landlords fear that they will lose their land altogether if the laws are enforced or, worse, extended. So, in anticipation of the new laws, they decide to do without tenants and employ landless or migrant labour. Often they mechanise, so that fewer people work on the land than did before.

79. Buying out landlords with national or international funds is often proposed as a way of solving land problems. However, the compensated landlord can wield new financial power and can, thus, still control rural people's lives. With the money from his land he can finance the merchants who

buy up the peasants' produce, he can provide funds for the moneylenders, or he can take up one of these roles himself. He may also start to exert financial power over urban people's lives by financing or establishing processing plants for agricultural goods. Paid-off landlords do not disappear simply because they have ceased to be landlords.

80. Zimbabwe is one of the few places where landlords would actually leave the country if they were paid off. But if that happens they will still not cease to exist; there is a danger that they will repeat their role in Latin America, where several governments have already offered large tracts of land and other inducements to former Rhodesian settlers.

81. Land reforms are liable to disrupt agricultural production while they are taking place. To a poor country government this is quite a disincentive to reform. One proposal made regularly at international fora is that a consortium of governments or the World Bank should offer to 'insure' land reform programmes (or at least those which meet certain internationally agreed criteria). The most common proposal is to guarantee to supply food, on a diminishing scale over a period of years, during the changeover to a new land tenure scheme. This type of scheme would be highly unlikely to produce just, egalitarian land reform if used as a bribe to induce reluctant governments to undertake reform, or as a tool to retain in power governments favourable to those providing the funds. An 'insurance' programme could well be useful if rural people, supported by the urban workers and a truly representative government, had already decided for themselves what they wanted to achieve. But it is probable that such a movement would not want outside interference and would reject such aid because they doubted the motive behind it.

82. While one attitude to land reform is that it is a panacea, at the other extreme is the attitude that the idea should be dismissed because it is too violent. It is sometimes possible to achieve land reform without violence but it is impossible to put off land reform and at the same time avoid violence. Peasant movements and associations are repressed wherever there is a land problem and this repression is itself violence. Oxfam files are full of reports of violence by landlords on tenants and labourers. People living on the land are moved out by gangs of armed thugs, or by the police or the army, even when, in theory, the law supports the tenants. It is not only private landlords who can hire such violent means of repression. Large firms, both national and international, act similarly, sometimes with government support. The courts support landowners too. In India, 300,000 of the 1.5 million crimes registered in 1978 involved land disputes. [22]

It is little wonder that peasants, thus oppressed, resort to violence themselves. They may try to seize land by force or they may plunder the landlord's crops at harvest time. They are taking what they consider is theirs by right. It is not a question of avoiding violence by avoiding land reform. Existing land tenure systems breed violence. The only way violence can be reduced is through more egalitarian and, therefore, more just land tenure systems.

83.   Another view which is closely linked to a fear of violence is the idea that land reform would not be necessary anywhere if population numbers could be reduced and thus "alleviate the pressure on land and the accompanying threat of discontented people". Although birth rates are beginning to fall, population numbers will increase for some time yet and the 'population explosion' is certainly a matter for concern in certain areas of the world. However, until people can be sure that their children will survive, it makes sense for them to have a large number so that someone is there to take care of them in old age. Studies have shown that infant mortality is much higher among families with no land to subsist on than among those families with even a little land. [23] It is a very vicious circle.

84.   Landlessness, poverty, malnutrition and birth rate are all closely linked; to concentrate on reducing population ignores the root cause of poverty which is unequal division of the resources for agricultural production. The problem in most countries is not so much a general overcrowding of land, but the control of most land by a few, leaving little for the many.

85.   Some people think land reform will not be needed in the future because new technical innovations in agriculture will increase food supplies. This is similar to the idea that reducing populations is a solution in itself. Increased food production does not help the poor unless they can actually eat the produce, and that is unlikely to happen unless they earn enough money to buy the food they need or, better still, have control over the agricultural resources.

86.   Described below are some examples of efforts towards land reform taken both by governments and by rural people. Nearly every developing country has introduced a programme which it has described as land reform. However, most of them have produced negligible results because they have not been designed to change the power structure. Only a very few countries have achieved this.

Examples of `Land Reform' in Latin America

87.   Countries where profound reform took place were Mexico (following the revolution of 1910), Bolivia (after 1952), Cuba (after 1959), Chile (between 1964 and 1973), and Peru (under the military Government from 1968). These reforms varied in their causes, impact and duration. Cuba and, to a

lesser extent, Chile attempted a socialist solution, the former under a Marxist-Leninist, one-party State, the latter within the institutions of liberal democracy. In Mexico and Bolivia agrarian reform came as part of a process of political and social change initiated by a 'populist' movement. In Peru the reform was to a large extent legislated into existence by a progressive-minded military Government.

88. Most governments paid at least lip-service to land reform during the 1960s. In large part this was the result of pressure by the United States through President Kennedy's Alliance for Progress, the programme of aid for Latin America for the decade of the 1960s. A condition of this programme of aid was the preparation by the recipient country of a plan for land reform which had as its main aim the subdivision of unproductive large estates. The plan was to establish a class of family farmers which (it was hoped) would be more efficient and lay the foundations of political stability in the countryside. The USA was afraid that a second Cuba might develop in Latin America. The intention of their aid was to stop this happening.

89. The result of this programme was a series of national plans which for the most part remained on paper. In those that were implemented, only a small sector of the rural population was affected, mainly by settling farmers on previously unoccupied land in colonisation schemes. In at least one case — that of Venezuela — reform involved the widespread purchase of land for distribution. The price paid to landowners was extremely favourable and this 'reform' has been seen as little more than a bonus for the landowning class and a means of payment to the peasant clients of the two main political parties.

90. Several conclusions are suggested by these experiences of land reform in Latin America. One is that rural organisations which represented the beneficiaries of reform were commonly only a part, and frequently only a minor part, of the coalitions of interest behind the reforming government. Peru is the best example here; although the military initiated widespread changes in the countryside, the regime was reluctant to devolve power to the organisations of peasants and rural workers. As a result, these organisations were powerless to resist the consequences of the coup of 1975 when the new military leaders began to dismantle or abandon the institutions created by the land reform.

91. Reforming governments face powerful opposition to radical change in the countryside. The example of Chile shows how landowners, businessmen and their military allies may resort to extra-constitutional means to obtain their ends, resulting in a coup in the names of anti-communism and free enterprise. Since 1973 most of the land in Chile affected by the reforming

Christian Democrat and Popular Unity governments has been sold to private interests.

92.   This is not to say that the obstacles facing a reformist government are solely political. One must recognise that major reform involves great expense, at least in the short-term, both in the cost of establishing essential services (such as credit and agricultural extension services) and in the likelihood that food prices may rise immediately after reform.

93.   It will be interesting to study the way in which Nicaragua carries through its plans for reform in the next few years. Since July 1979 there has been a major change in the approach to land tenure. Most of the big landowners fled from Nicaragua when the Somoza Government fell to the Sandanistas. The aim in the rural areas in Nicaragua after the revolution was to ensure joint peasant ownership of the land and where possible to avoid State ownership. The sale or rent of land has been forbidden. Most of the available information comes from Leon Province but the indications are that the same type of organisational reform is being established throughout Nicaragua. [24]

94.   In Leon Province an effort has been made not to break up existing large estates but rather to hand them over to communes of families who will continue to farm them as large units. Each commune has an assembly containing one member from each family. The assembly appoints a communal board who undertake daily planning and evaluation. The plan is to rotate jobs at three monthly intervals to ensure that people are not corrupted by the power which some jobs would give them. Many of these families were previously landless labourers on the estates so their new control of agricultural resources is a very major change. Advisers are being provided to help them with techniques and decision-making where necessary. At present there is a team of fifty advisers in Leon Province.

95.   Crop patterns are not being changed much initially, although more emphasis had been put on local food crops than export crops. In most communes families are able to farm a small plot for their own immediate needs, usually vegetables and poultry.

96.   Some communes are much better endowed than others and a Federation of Communes has been organised to transfer surpluses between wealthy and poor communes. So far about 2,500 families have joined communes in Leon.

97.   Not all the land has been given to communes. At present small landowning peasants are continuing as before and large, State-owned estates are being operated by paid workers who, however, do have some say in the

operation. This is an area which the Government does not feel competent to alter at present.

Examples of 'Land Reform' in Asia

98. The best known examples of land reform in Asia have been in China and South Korea. There are some interesting comparisons to be made between these.

99. China is one of the best examples of a land reform which has really benefited the vast majority of the population. In a lengthy and often violent revolution, land was forcibly taken out of the control of the landowning minorities. Now the land is worked by cooperative groups in communes. Starvation and malnutrition have been largely eliminated.

100. China is one of the few developing countries which has managed to achieve economic advance while simultaneously reducing inequality and raising the standard of living of the vast majority of the population in the countryside. China has only 8% of the world's cultivable land but 20% of the world's population, about 800 million people. It is no mean feat to see that everyone is fed, clothed, housed, medically treated and educated. This has all been achieved through a strong political motivation which pervades the whole society.

101. Sartaj Aziz says, "China has gone far beyond the narrow concept of social justice; it has created a society which provides a sense of dignity, the spirit of self-reliance and the opportunity of participation and decision-making. Above all, it has brought about a fundamental change in values and objectives of development, with greater emphasis on collective rather than individual rewards and on social rather than purely materialistic or technological objectives. Material incentives are present and important, but they are secondary and subservient to social and political objectives. These achievements were not without cost, pitfalls and mistakes but, for such a large country as China, the achievements of the past twenty-seven years speak for themselves." [25]

102. Sartaj Aziz is very much in favour of the Chinese system but many people with different political leanings criticise the Chinese system because, they say, it removes personal freedom. But they have to admit that the people are far better off now than they were before the Revolution. In whatever direction China goes in the future (and there are indications that it is now on a more capitalist path), this does not detract from the fact that the society that exists today was founded on social justice.

103. An example of a capitalist country achieving land reform without a revolution is South Korea, which is commonly considered to have accomplished an economic miracle. Advocates of the free market system declare it a model for development. Opponents argue that its spectacular growth has been achieved at the expense of its workers and at the cost of political freedom and social development. Certainly the land reform which took place between 1948 and 1957 has left South Korea with a rural society more equal, more productive and more generally prosperous than any other non-communist developing country in Asia. From an acute dependence on rice imports it is now self-sufficient.

104. The question that should be asked about South Korea is how have its considerable achievements been reached? Does it offer a real way of escape for all, by capitalist means, from rural and urban poverty? South Korea's rural development emerged from exceptional circumstances. The USA, fearing the spread of Chinese communism, put pressure on South Korea to make changes which would alleviate rural unrest. One of the measures proposed was redistribution of land with Government compensation for the landlords paid by the USA. South Korea is still heavily dependent on the USA. The South Korean Government, with American support, has had to continue economic intervention; however, several reports, among them one from the World Council of Churches, [26] now say that inequalities are creeping back into the system. For example, tenancies are increasing and infringements of human rights are occurring regularly. This is because the system is at odds with the form of economic policy pursued in the industrial sector. It is questionable whether an economic and political structure essentially tied to unchecked capitalism is capable of shaping a system which in the long term benefits all members of society.

105. India has experienced a series of attempts at land reform but for the most part they have only been paper reforms. Rural people have no way of enforcing their legal rights because they are mostly illiterate and unaware that the law exists.

106. In the main, India's land reform programmes have been promoted by middle and upper class groups which genuinely want to see an improvement in the well-being of the peasant cultivators and landless people. They have little control, however, over the landlordism at village level. In practice, the amount of implementation of land reform measures has varied widely between states but in general, the social system has remained unaltered. Ceilings for landholding have been reduced and tenancy systems have been revised, but there are numerous ways in which landlords can evade these laws. Inequalities in land distribution in India are still vast.

107.   Reallocation of land does not often take place because the tenants are not
         sure of their rights and can often be intimidated by their landlords. The
         landowners can procrastinate. Land ceilings can be manipulated so that
         every member of the landlord's family (and even dogs, cats and buffaloes)
         own a piece of land below the ceiling level. [27]

         These two points are well illustrated by an Indian writer.

         "The dynamics of land reforms (ie redistribution) can be seen from
         the case of Rajasthan. A committee to fix ceilings on landholdings
         was set up in November 1953. It took four years to submit the
         report. Another two passed to push through the legislation. In
         March 1960, the President's assent was obtained. Another three
         and a half years went by before the draft rules were framed. On the
         eve of its implementation in December 1963, the landlords went to
         the Court of Law. After they lost the case, April 1, 1965 was set as
         the date of enforcement to be postponed until October 1965. Then
         came some operational problems raised by the landlords. Came the
         1967 general elections and so land reforms had to wait. In the mean-
         while, the *mala fide* land transfers up to December 1969 were
         legalised. Thus the saga that began in 1953 came to its climax in
         1970 by which time the bulk of the surplus land had been spirited
         away. This is by no means an exceptional case." [28]

108.   In the sixth Indian Five Year Plan are some very clear facts on the failures
         of past efforts to bring about a more equitable realisation of rural assets,
         especially land, even though legally there are fixed ceilings on land holdings
         in all the Indian states.

109.   The plan estimates that the area of surplus land still held by owners in
         excess of the ceilings fixed by law is more than 21 million acres. Yet the
         state governments (land distribution is a state subject) have estimated only
         5.32 million acres to be available for distribution. The area 'taken over' by
         the state governments for redistribution is only 2.1 million acres, and the
         area actually distributed is only 1.29 million acres, 5% of the area which
         should have been distributed under the laws on holdings. [29]

110.   One of the most interesting attempts at land reform in India was under-
         taken by a voluntary movement, Bhoodan — the Land Gift Movement —
         which began in 1951. It was initiated by one man, Vinobha Bhave, who
         was a disciple of Gandhi. The aim was to solve the problem of landlessness.
         He walked through India appealing to landowners to donate one sixth of
         their holdings to the poor and landless. His aim was to collect 50 million
         acres to distribute to 10 million landless families by 1957. Many other
         Gandhians supported his appeal, but by 1957 less than 5 million acres

were acquired and some of it later reverted to its original owners. Nonetheless, the acquisition of gifts of 5 million acres was still a very remarkable achievement. The problems lay in the fact that the land which was donated was mostly of poor quality and the families which settled on it did not receive help in the form of implements, money or training, to develop the land.

111.   After 1957 a new movement grew out of the Bhoodan idea. This was known as the Gramdan movement and has been far more popular. The emphasis has been on a new pattern of community life, rather than on merely redistributing the land. The idea was that farmers should give their land to the village so that all land could be cultivated communally. For the purpose of Gramdan, ownership is distinguished from possession (ie right to use it). Any owner of land may donate all his land, subject to the condition that he shall not continue to possess more than nineteen twentieths of it. In joining Gramdan the owner surrenders ownership of the entire area and also possession (ie use) of one twentieth of the land, this proportion being used for redistribution to the landless in the village.

112.   The original idea of wholly Gramdan villages has been greatly weakened in order to make it work. A village can now call itself a Gramdan community provided that half its land has been donated in Gramdan and that at least three quarters of both owners and residents have joined the movement. [30]

Land Reform in Africa

113.   There have not been the same sort of land reforms in Africa that have occurred in Latin America and Asia. There have, however, been changes in landholding systems which many people would claim are against the interests of poor rural farmers, and particularly against the interests of women.

114.   For example, in Kenya in a pre-colonial pastoral and agricultural economy, women were usually able to protect their own interests; they had the common right to use land for grazing which was far more secure than any form of individual ownership because it was the equal inalienable right of everyone.

115.   When land registration was introduced into Kenya, women lost many of their land rights. The western concept of individual ownership went hand in hand with giving land-title to the head of the household, 'the man'. Once land could be bought, mortgaged and sold it opened the way for people to acquire more land. The more successful farmer could thus buy from the less successful and land could be lost through debt.

116. Improvements in agricultural techniques, introduced through foreign aid and by foreign experts, have been mainly directed to men: tractors were given to men, training in new techniques was given to men, replacement of livestock was to men only. All this has compounded women's second-class status in many parts of Africa.

117. The Tanzanian experience shows how land and its benefits can be fairly allocated without having to give every man his little patch to buy and sell. In Tanzania land is no longer a commodity which can be bought and sold. It belongs to the people and to the State. Anyone in a rural area must farm a set minimum acreage. Villages have some communal crop areas and some land which is farmed by individuals and families. But they do not own the land and cannot sell it. If they do not farm the land allocated to them by their village committee it can be given to someone else. Although Tanzania is a very poor country, it has managed to share its admittedly low production benefits thinly but relatively evenly amongst its people, in sharp contrast with Kenya where there are far greater disparities between the rich and the poor. Given the same political will, it would be possible for most African countries to adopt the same egalitarian policies as Tanzania.

118. The plans for independent Zimbabwe point to a more egalitarian society and fairer land sharing. In a policy statement, Prime Minister Mugabe has said that resettlement of refugees, both internal and external, was high on the list of his Government's priorities. He said that the policy would be to settle the people on a collective basis on unused (former white) land through a programme of cooperatives and collectives. He stated that there was plenty of unused and under-utilised land which could be acquired immediately for resettlement.

119. Oxfam Field Staff in Zimbabwe have reported that the new Government intends to resettle the displaced population in a planned fashion based on its long-term policy for rural development. It will take advantage of the fact that there are so many displaced people to set up self-sustaining rural communities, rather than leave them to return home and await an eventual assistance programme. This is an extremely encouraging development and one in which Oxfam will seek to participate as fully as possible.

4 Can Official Aid and Investment Benefit the Rural Poor?

120. During the last two decades there has been a dramatic increase in the number of poor people in the world which cannot be accounted for purely by the increase in population. A higher percentage of the world's population is now below the poverty line, as defined by organisations such as the World Bank. Several studies illustrate this point. One concerns the number of people below the poverty line in five states in India, and four other Asian countries. The graph overleaf, taken from this study, shows that the incidence of rural poverty increased, sometimes very substantially, everywhere except in Pakistan and Andhra Pradesh.

121. Yet, during the same period, all these countries (except Bangladesh) achieved substantial growth. At first sight this combination of simultaneously increasing growth and poverty is rather startling. How can it be explained? What seems to happen is that growth itself exacerbates poverty within a society which already has an unequal distribution of wealth. The benefits of growth accrue to people according to their wealth and their position in the power structure. Those who start with little or nothing are left behind and drop deeper into poverty. To him that has, more shall be given, as St. Luke and a hundred proverbs across the world have it.

122. The most powerful people in a rural society are those who have control over the most land. So investment in the rural sector inevitably benefits the landholders and the more land they hold, the more it benefits them. They are able to use their increased wealth to buy more land and to mechanise. The result is more landless people and fewer jobs.

123. The effect is the same whether the investment leading to growth is generated internally (an average of 80% of Third World development funds are local) or from outside (in the form of commercial investment or aid). This Chapter concentrates on inputs from external sources — inputs which it is easy to assume reduce poverty because that is what one is led to believe they do. In practice, though, they contribute to growth which, in an unequal society, contributes to the causes of poverty.

124. Rapid economic growth is seen by many, particularly in the UN, to be the best way of eliminating poverty. In the agricultural sector 'moderni-

INCREASE IN INCIDENCE OF RURAL POVERTY 1956-1975

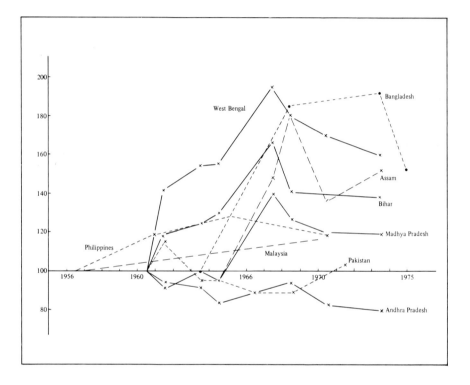

Source: Keith Griffin and Azizur Rahman Khan, "Poverty in the Third World: Ugly Facts and Fancy Models". *World Development*, Vol. 6, No. 3, March 1978, pp 295 – 303.

sation' is the key word. The implication is that until now the rural poor have been left behind in the process of modernisation. All that needs to be done is to draw them into it. In practice this is a self-defeating aim; the poor remain poor because they have little access to the productive resources of land and water. Often modernisation itself makes them poorer by strengthening the resources of the rich.

125. It is the people who are, in effect, the victims of this process that Oxfam tries to support and with whom it tries to work. Thus, while the major aid agencies aim to increase growth, Oxfam works with the victims of growth, the people who are at the bottom of the power structure. Support is specifically directed towards the needs which people have defined themselves, towards development in which they participate and make their own decisions.

126. The major international, governmental aid agencies work through national governments and thus depend on these governments' priorities for the direction of aid. Most economies in the Third World are not designed to benefit the poor, and, as has been shown, do not in fact do so. And most governments either will not or cannot change this. They consist of people who benefit from (or represent people who benefit from) the economy as it is. They do not wish to change it. Even if they did, they would find that governments which have developed one system may not be powerful enough to change to another involving a different distribution of the benefits of the economy.

127. The major international and governmental aid agencies do not give priority to helping the poor against their own governments. Bilateral aid (government-to-government) is largely concerned with trade, defence, diplomatic support, etc. In the case of Britain these concerns are to be increased; the current Foreign Secretary has announced: "We believe it is right at the present time to give greater weight in the allocation of our aid to political, industrial and commercial considerations alongside our basic developmental objectives."[31] Oxfam regards this as a retrograde step in the development of Britain's aid policy. Multilateral aid (through the UN and similar international agencies) is less closely connected to national policies, but even this aid is directed by member governments, so they, too, do little to help people at the bottom of the Third World power structure.

128. The myth that poverty can be eliminated through economic growth is sustained by the great majority of world press comment. Journalists reflect the standard assumptions of the rich countries — that more food means fewer hungry people, that poor countries benefit from their relationship with the rich, that more aid means less poverty, that economic growth is good. With some notable exceptions, most journalists take on

trust what they are told about development projects; they tend to report an increase in agricultural production, for example, rather than how many people have got into debt or have been made landless as a result of an aid project. The poor cannot get the ear of the media and so these myths remain unchallenged.

The World Bank

129. The International Bank for Reconstruction and Development (IBRD), generally known as the World Bank, is the largest single lender for agricultural development in the world and its influence on development is far-reaching since it also has close links with other development agencies of the UN, bilateral donors and also with private enterprise.

130. The World Bank is a proponent of development through economic growth and modernisation, but in 1973 Robert McNamara, the President of the World Bank, stated: "The basic problem of poverty and growth in the developing world can be stated very simply. The growth is not equitably reaching the poor." [32]

131. Since 1973 the World Bank has concentrated on lending in the rural sector and its International Development Association (IDA) has directed its soft loans (those offering easy terms) particularly to investment in the rural areas. The World Bank itself admits, however, that it can do little for the poor unless it is investing in countries which have opted for more equal, participative development. In 1973, McNamara said: "The sad truth is that in most countries, the centralised administration of scarce resources — both money and skills — has usually resulted in most of them being allocated to a small group of the rich and powerful." [33]

132. Despite its evident awareness of this fact, the Bank continues to invest in countries where economic development is likely to increase the gap between rich and poor. Although McNamara has identified the problem, World Bank policies are reinforcing current systems. Part of the confusion about development aims comes from the definition of 'poor'. The 'poor' which the World Bank aids are people who have some resources (such as land) at their disposal and who, the Bank believes, could create jobs for poorer people, given a growth economy. It is the relationship between the people defined as 'poor' by the World Bank, and the poorest of the poor, which needs to be explored.

133. The World Bank funds the middle-level farmer with perhaps five to twenty hectares of land and by doing this is reinforcing the process of differentiation. Because these farmers are encouraged to provide food for the towns, they enter the market and need a money income to buy more agricultural

equipment. They accumulate wealth and it is thus concentrated into fewer and fewer hands. Those who are unable to compete sell up and move into towns. The size of each farming unit increases and tenants and sharecroppers are often thrown off the land and become landless, as revealed by the examples quoted below of projects in Brazil and Indonesia.

134. Obviously Oxfam is not able to comment on all 570 projects in the World Bank's agricultural programme. Indeed, even when criticism would seem to be justified it would be difficult to prove that the situation prior to World Bank influence has been worsened because of their presence. Attention can only be drawn to the adverse effects of World Bank projects on the poor people Oxfam is trying to help in those cases reported by Oxfam Field Staff.

For example, one Field Officer in Brazil wrote in his annual report:

> "The World Bank pours vast sums into Brazil, one of its largest borrowers, and consequently has a great deal of potential influence over the policies of Government agencies. Yet only in a small number of cases has this power been used to lessen human suffering caused by the implementation of grandiose projects. One is led to the inescapable conclusion that for these bodies the interests of the masses are marginal at best, irrelevant at worst. The reality contrasts too often with the public image put forward by development agencies. The World Bank's 'Assault on Poverty' campaign is a case in point. Political expediency continues to be the order of the day, and as long as the poor have no voice it will continue to be so." [34]

135. In Gujarat, India, Oxfam's Field Director has been requested to give legal aid to a group of Adivasi people to fight for their land which was threatened by an improvement and irrigation scheme about to be implemented by the World Bank. [35] Such problems caused by large, multilateral aid institutions are frequently mentioned in Oxfam Field Staff reports.

The Food and Agriculture Organisation (FAO)

136. The FAO devotes much of its publicity to explaining how it is helping to relieve the problems of hunger. The FAO is an excellent technical agency but as such it approaches all the problems of hunger, land and food with technical solutions such as improved irrigation and better varieties of seed. Many critics consider that the FAO should employ more people sensitive to the social and political factors which cause hunger. Even if this became FAO policy, its power to aid the poor would still be limited.

137. The FAO was created to serve the interests of its member governments. It has to present an acceptable, non-political image to all of them. It cannot,

therefore, make a direct attack on hunger because in many cases that would involve the FAO aligning itself with opponents of the very governments it serves. The FAO, like all UN agencies, has to wait for requests from governments. It cannot send uninvited missions to study problems of hunger. Many of the member governments of the FAO are not representative of the majority of their people and they would resist such studies being made. All these limitations have long been recognised but the FAO has now become a self-perpetuating machine. There are many individual employees within the organisation genuinely seeking to eradicate the causes of hunger but within the framework of the FAO they have a difficult task.

138. The effect of the FAO on government agricultural policies should not be underestimated. It has often acted as a reinforcement to the status quo in countries where it has worked. For example, the Indicative World Plan which the FAO produced in 1969/70 put heavy emphasis on increasing production through mechanisation. The result has been greater production certainly, but for whom? Many rural tenants have lost their plots as landlords have thrown them off in order to mechanise and many seasonal labourers no longer have work. Statistics on the number of people thrown out of work by mechanisation are not usually available because governments are not keen to collect information that is against their political interests.

139. Some figures are available, however. In Western Java a large power tilling machine can eliminate 2,000 days of work per year for village labourers and divert $2,650 to the owner-dealer and manufacturer. A World Bank report warns that these tillers could eliminate more than a million jobs. It quotes a Javanese worker: "The only people who like tractors are the ones who own them." [36] Unless a society is already organised in a way that allows the benefits of growth to reach all its people, any technical improvement will always benefit the richer and stronger members of society more than the poor.

Infrastructure for Agriculture

140. When roads and dams are built through official aid and investment, they are built to improve the possibilities for economic growth within the countries concerned. Often the aid or investment agencies involved are organisations which, in their literature, talk about helping or reaching the poorest. While land tenure is unequal, however, any new service to the land automatically accrues to the landowner, rather than to his tenants or labourers. Therefore, these services become additional support mechanisms for the existing power structures.

141.   Provision of irrigation to increase crop yields and to allow more land to come under cultivation is a good example of the type of aid which appears to be very desirable. But from the poor peasant's point of view what is important is the socio-political context into which such irrigation programmes are introduced because it is that which will determine whether he benefits or not.

142.   A case study which describes such a situation is that of the provision of a dam in Brazil. A study in 1975 made by an Oxfam adviser analysed the results of three irrigation projects, two in the State of Paraiba and one in Ceara, on a tributary of the Jaguaribe River. [37] All had been operating for at least two years and two were regarded as 'showpieces' of the irrigation programme. The procedures and objectives were roughly similar: the land which was to be irrigated was expropriated, with compensation paid only to landowners. Tenants or sharecroppers received nothing and some owners who were unable to prove their titles were also forced off their land without compensation. No provision was made for relocating or assisting in any way the dispossessed.

143.   The selection of those who were to be given irrigated plots, was quite elaborate. Eligibility to join the project was based on a variety of factors, viz, the farmer had to be the head of a family, be aged between 19 and 49, be of Brazilian nationality, have made his living only in agriculture, have insufficient land for a decent living, have lived in the same place for three years and he and his family had to be of 'proven good conduct'. Priority was supposed to be given first, to ex-landowners, second, to farmers who previously worked in the area, and finally, to landless workers. Within these classes, preference was supposed to be given first, to those from the area expropriated, second, to those from neighbouring parts of the valley, third, to those from drier areas of the surrounding semi-arid highlands, and fourth, from other strategic areas. In addition, the project directors were allowed to recommend not more than 10% of applicants outside these categories.

144.   In the three cases studied, far fewer farmers were eventually accommodated on the projects than had been displaced. The Sume project, for example, comprises 260 hectares, of which half is irrigated and the remainder utilised in common for pasture. Before expropriation, 73 families lived in the valley, of which 47 were smallholders. 26 families are now accommodated and 9 more will be when the project is completed — a total of 35 instead of the original 73. The creation of permanent jobs in the rural sector was one of the three major objectives of the irrigation programme in north-east Brazil. The study found that only one livelihood was 'created' for every two or three livelihoods that were lost.

145. The second objective was to increase family incomes substantially through cultivating high value crop for sale. The incomes which the new settlers have achieved are not very encouraging for the Brazilian Government. Many of the settlers are still making a loss.

146. The third objective was to increase agricultural production. However, except on the Sume project, it has not proved possible to grow and commercialise high value crops on a significant scale.

147. This programme was heavily supported by the World Bank and other investment agencies through the Brazilian Government. In spite of the meagre returns to the existing projects, at very high social and economic cost, there appears to have been no reconsideration of the programme, which has been extended to the Lower Sao Francisco Valley with very similar results and consequences.

148. Although a feasibility study indicated that the second phase would be as harmful to the rural people as the first, in 1975 the World Bank allocated $56.5 million (£28m) to the scheme and paid out $23 million (£11.5m) that year. In its annual report, the World Bank stated: "Important elements of agrarian reform incorporated in the project will help ensure the equitable sharing of benefits." [38]

149. Oxfam Field Staff witnessed the devastation caused to the peasants when work started in the Sao Francisco Valley. The tenant smallholders and sharecroppers were unwilling to leave because no provisions had been made either to compensate them or to resettle them. They were cleared off the land by armed men while the bulldozers came in and destroyed their homes. Most of these people drifted to the cities because there was nowhere else to go. In August 1977, Oxfam's Field Director reported that 1,200 families had been displaced to make room for 200 irrigation farmers.

150. In 1976/77 Oxfam made two grants to assist a Diocesan team formed to help small farmers who were threatened with summary eviction from their lands by the Government irrigation agency CODEVASF. As a result of the work of this team, a court decided to award compensation to 286 evicted farmers and the decision was later supported in the Supreme Court.

151. In spite of the criticisms of the social effects of such projects, both the World Bank and other multilateral and bilateral investment and aid agencies continue to implement similar schemes without due concern for the people they will affect. In another example there have been massive peasant demonstrations in the Philippines about the planned Chico River Dam which threatens the life of the Kalinga Bontoc people. The dam will cover their hand-built rice terraces in order to provide electric power

2.1 The problem in most countries is control of most land by a few: gardening on marginal land, Bolivia.

2.2 Land and water are usually the basis for power in developing countries: levelling land for paddy, Tamil Nadu, India.

2.3 *The goal is a genuine sharing of control: campesinos working in formation to facilitate irrigation, Peru.*

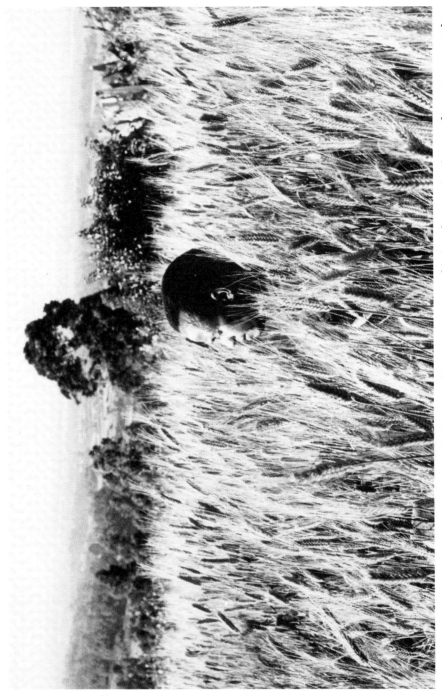

2.4 *There is nothing intrinsically wrong with the idea of increasing crop yields but the question is one of power, not merely technology: an abundance of grain, Ethiopia.*

for rich urban people. This particular group of peasants hold the land communally and are self-sufficient in food. They produce enough surplus crops to earn the cash necessary to purchase tools and housing materials. [39]

152.   Other kinds of irrigation which would seem to be more direct and appropriate have also been found to enrich landowners. The World Bank's IDA division loaned $444 million (£222m) to a project in Bangladesh, a quarter of which was for irrigation. One of the 3,000 deep tubewells was installed in a village where some Oxfam-America contacts were living. The tubewell was supposed to belong the the farmers' cooperative but in reality was owned by the biggest landlord in the area. The aid for irrigation, therefore, increased his power.

153.   This was not an isolated incident. A foreign expert told Oxfam-America researchers: "100% of the wells are going to the big boys." The Swedish International Development Authority (SIDA), which had helped to finance the project, made an evaluation of 270 tubewells. Their report states: "It is not surprising that the tubewells have been situated on the land of the well-to-do farmers, or that it is the same well-to-do farmers who are the chairmen and the managers of the irrigation groups. It would have been more surprising if the tubewells had not been located on their land, with the existing rural power structure, maintained largely because of the unequal distribution of the land."

154.   The World Bank itself, although it has claimed to be paying attention to small farmers getting some benefits, has to admit: "In a project such as this where the major result is to increase the productivity of the land, to a large extent the distribution of direct benefits must reflect the existing land ownership pattern." [40]

155.   A danger of introducing irrigation and better crop methods to subsistence farmers is that they will go into debt and become landless. The British Government has funded an irrigation project using underground water in the barren Gunung Kidul area of southern Central Java in Indonesia. The scheme is relatively small compared with the Bangladesh scheme described above. According to Oxfam contacts, local farmers were at first reluctant to use water from the 28 tubewells, some of which lay idle for as much as three years. When the opening ceremony was due, the local 'regent' threatened to sack all village heads who could not persuade farmers to use the irrigation water. So by the time the project was officially opened, over half the area of 1,270 hectares was under irrigation.

156.   But the farmers still have doubts about the irrigation scheme which they consider has been imposed on them. The problem is that the Gunung Kidul irrigation scheme, like others of its type, is part of a 'package'

rice intensification programme in which farmers are forced to accept credit in the form of fertilisers, insecticides, working capital and high yielding rice varieties in order to produce yields great enough to be able to pay the high running-cost of the diesel pumps. These high yielding rice varieties, however, are very vulnerable to infestations of rats and insect pests such as the brown leaf-hopper. The farmers are afraid that if they get into debt through crop losses from pest attacks they will be forced to sell their livestock, household possessions and even their land in order to clear their debts.

157. Their fears are not without foundation; in Java landlessness is rapidly increasing. About 7 million households (nearly half the total) are landless or almost landless. They depend on irregular work as agricultural labourers or try to find work in towns in construction work or similar jobs. Another indicator of the increasing poverty in Java is the decreasing calorie intake levels among the bottom 40% of the rural population. It would seem that the rush of loans and grants into Indonesia is not helping the poorest members of the population and may indeed be contributing to their poverty.[41]

Modernisation of Agriculture

158. Modernising agriculture in order to increase productivity seems, on the face of it, to be a way of feeding more people. But, as illustrated in Chapter 2, improvements to productivity can actually be harmful to the poor if introduced into certain social and political situations. Take, for example, the story of the Green Revolution, which is a good example of technical inputs introduced into an unequal system of land holding, thereby reinforcing or even increasing the gap between rich and poor people.

159. The published aim of the Green Revolution scientists was to increase grain yields without the necessity of expanding cultivated crop areas. Undoubtedly they saw their work as a contribution to 'feeding the hungry'. New dwarf plants described as High Yielding Varieties (HYVs) were developed which could produce vastly more grain than traditional varieties. However, the HYVs could only be grown with applications of fertiliser and with the provision of good irrigation. They were also far less resistant to disease than traditional varieties and so needed applications of fungicides and pesticides. If all these inputs were not available, the seeds were likely to produce a lower yield than the traditional varieties.

160. The HYVs were pioneered in Mexico, and then introduced into India, Pakistan, and Turkey during the 1960s. The Rockefeller and Ford Foundations, which had funded the original work, stated that they hoped that

the world food crisis was solved. Enough food could be produced for all the world's population. Hunger would soon be a thing of the past. This ignored the fact that hungry people are poor people and do not have the kind of purchasing power needed either to buy the food produced or to buy the means to produce it themselves.

161.   Susan George points out that behind the publicity drive for the Green Revolution were many multinational companies which were expecting to make high profits from their sales of fertilisers and pesticides and later from the sales of advanced agricultural equipment; they were concerned with profits rather than with feeding the hungry. [42]

162.   The negative effects on poor rural people have been numerous. Perhaps the best way to understand these effects is to consider one particular country. India's experience of the Green Revolution is typical of the problems encountered by other countries. HYVs were introduced into India in 1966. The contrast between the practice of cultivating these new seeds and typical practices of traditional subsistence or near-subsistence agriculture can be seen easily. Traditionally, an Indian peasant family would save their own seed; fertiliser would be supplied by manure from their animals; the family would consume the major part of their crop. They would be dependent only marginally on the market and often such cash as they required would be supplied by part-time work for wages, selling chickens, vegetable produce, milk, etc. Usually a complex system of inter-family or clan supports provided insurance against individual crop failures or other disasters.

163.   The change to cultivating the new varieties has involved an exposure to many risks and uncertainties not previously encountered. The hybrid seeds, fertilisers and pesticides must be bought at the beginning of each season, and must be available when required. Enough of the crop must be sold at a sufficiently high price to cover these costs and to leave a margin that warrants the extra risk and effort involved. Since very poor Indian peasants have no capital to invest in such expenditure, they are dependent on credit for their purchases and interest charges must also be covered by the eventual sale of the surplus crop. Other risks include the high vulnerability to pest and disease attacks on the new varieties. After expensive outlays, the peasant farmer could lose a large part of his crop.

164.   Peasants do not have access to the resources necessary to grow these varieties successfully. Attempts by the Indian Government to provide these resources have failed consistently, largely because the distributing agencies have almost always been dominated by the richer and more powerful families in the community, who succeed in diverting the benefits of Government programmes to themselves. The hierarchical nature of

village life, with rigid stratification along caste and social lines, has reinforced the economic power of the larger landowners. [43]

165.   So the poor farmers cannot escape from their poverty. At the same time, the success of the already richer farmers has led to an increase in their wealth and influence and hence in their ability to control the land. The rich have increased the size of their land-holdings and the distribution of assets such as tubewells and tractors is now more unequal than it was before the introduction of the HYVs.

166.   There has also been an increase in the number of landless labourers. As the value of land to those able to afford the cultivation of the new varieties has increased, tenants and small landowners have been forced off their land by various legal and illegal means. Others have lost their land by getting into debt while attempting to grow HYVs. In some cases, there has been a temporarily increased demand for labour to work on the farms, since the HYVs require intensive cultivation. This is particularly true when double cropping becomes possible as the result of the shorter growing period of the grains. But increased mechanisation has typically accompanied or followed the successful cultivation of the new crops, so that the initial demand for more labour is later offset by labour replacement and machinery, thus making people jobless as well as landless.

167.   As a recent study points out: "It (the Green Revolution) suggests there has been a major breakthrough in agricultural production, that this has been done in a peaceful context without the need for institutional reform, and indeed, that technical change is an alternative to political change . . . all of these suggestions are misleading." [44]

168.   It is clear that nothing is intrinsically wrong with the idea of increasing crop yields, and Oxfam supports projects using, for example, HYVs, but the question is one of power and not simply of technology. Where inequalities of land tenure and wealth exist, such innovations as the Green Revolution can only increase the gap. If the same innovations were to be introduced into a society which had, say, communal control of agricultural production then the benefits could be shared equally and questions such as the purchase of a tractor would be analysed on the basis of whether it would be for the common good to release some labour for other communal activities.

169.   The Green Revolution did not result in overall increased agricultural production or in reduced malnutrition. However, it has accelerated the development of a market-orientated capitalist agriculture. It has encouraged the growth of wage labour and thus helped to create, or at least augment, a class of agricultural labourers. It has increased the power of

landowners and contributed to the increasing conflict between rich and poor and also to the increasing income gap.

170. The Green Revolution has resulted in a massively uneven allocation of resources. In bypassing the need for structural reform in favour of a technical 'solution' to the problem of agricultural productivity, it has made a genuine land reform even less likely. It can now be seen to be essentially a short-term solution, and inadequate even in the short-term. The changes which have accompanied it have made it more difficult, if not impossible, to attack the basic problem of land reform and to achieve an equitable and efficient distribution of productive resources. The power of the present landowners has become almost unchallengeable. The failure of the Government even to impose a land tax on the beneficiaries of huge public expenditure on irrigation, credit subsidies, subsidised seed, fertilisers, etc, is an indication of their political power and influence.

Land Tenure and Food Aid

171. Food aid is often seen by the press and public as a goodwill, humanitarian gesture to people in need and Oxfam has shown its importance, for example, in its recent relief programme in Kampuchea. It should be remembered, however, that food aid is often an easy way for western governments to dispose of food surpluses in order to maintain reasonable prices to their farmers. For this reason, food aid is not always given in situations where it is really needed and often, instead of helping the rural poor, it can actually harm them. It can destroy local markets for their crops and further impoverish them, so that they have to sell their land or give up their tenancies and move to towns or work as landless labourers.

172. The negative impact of inappropriate food aid was well illustrated in Guatemala after the earthquake in 1976. Although housing, and not food stocks, had been destroyed, thousands of tons of food aid were sent in mainly from the USA. Handout queues had a demoralising effect upon people. The sharp drop in the price of maize was blamed in part on the distribution of food aid: "The people of the Highlands grow their maize, and if they have some left over from their needs, they sell it," explained Benito Sicajan Sipac, President of a cooperative from Chimaltenango. "When all that food came in, there was no longer a market for maize, and the farmers lost out." [45]

173. Food-for-work programmes (in which people are paid with food aid for their work) may seem a good way of providing employment for poor people. In practice these programmes tend to benefit the richer landlords and give only minor benefit to the people that actually carry out the work. The poor get food, but the long-term benefit accrues to the land-

owner. In north-west Haiti, an Oxfam researcher found that larger land-owners can apply to the USA agency CARE for food. They then hire labourers who receive food aid as their pay. Much of this food they then proceed to sell for cash in the local markets, in competition with the local small farmer. The Director of one food aid agency told the researcher that the day following food-for-work payments many farmers do not bother to send their produce to the market. [46]

174. Another problem with food-for-work in Haiti is that there is no follow-up maintenance. A large World Food Programme project in the south which operated from 1974-1978 on erosion control is now slowly falling to pieces: as the Haitians say, "No more food, no more work". It is of no interest to the peasant to maintain the terracing that was built since he does not own the land and there is no more food aid. The rich who do own it are not interested since they would now have to pay for up-keep themselves.

175. Oxfam believes that food aid is vital for emergency relief, refugees and similar groups of people, yet only about 20% of food aid is used for these purposes and is often hard to obtain since so much food is ear-marked for development projects or budgetary support, both of dubious value to the poor.

5 The Future Effects of Present International Attitudes to Poverty and Hunger: the World Conference on Agrarian Reform and Rural Development

176. The World Conference on Agrarian Reform and Rural Development (WCARRD), held in July 1979 under the auspices of the FAO, heavily confirmed the points made in the previous Chapter. Undoubtedly, the Conference has influenced policies and plans for the future among international decision makers, perhaps for the next decade. This does not bode well for the poor, landless people of the world.

177. Casual observers to the Conference might have been forgiven for imagining that this was a forum where at last the real causes of rural poverty would be exposed. But the Conference was not concerned with social justice for the poor, because it was an inter-governmental Conference and very few governments are seriously interested in such issues.

178. The official literature, both before and after the Conference, gave the impression that the Conference was about 'participation'. It implied that it is commonly accepted that 'we are all in this together' and that all that is needed is for the rural poor to become closely involved in the planning and implementation of future rural development strategies. In reality, many of the governments represented at the Conference are in direct conflict with the masses of rural people in their countries. In many parts of the Third World, whenever a group of peasants asserts its rights, even those enshrined in the legal code, it is rapidly repressed.

179. Although the official Conference literature discussed the need to reduce inequalities, delegates tended to concentrate on questions of economic growth in the agricultural sector and did not give much attention to the poor except as producers of wealth. Even if they had concentrated on reducing poverty, a world conference is not a suitable forum to discuss issues which are essentially social and political. Governments which are already politically motivated to undertake reforms that will genuinely involve peoples' participation did not need such a conference. Those that are not so motivated are unlikely to have been convinced by a conference

that they should change their position. It is even possible that the Conference may have had a negative effect; by concentrating on technical problems, it may have served to confirm the illusion that poverty is a technical, and not a social and political, issue.

180. The United Nations Research Institute for Social Development (UNRISD) writes in a critique of the WCARRD papers: "One could get the impression that the authors accept the common international convention that governments are interested in doing everything possible to improve the conditions of the rural poor and to push development, as the term is defined by the United Nations consensus, and that they are only waiting for the technicians to provide the proper recipes before implementing effective development policies." [47]

181. The key document for WCARRD was the 'Review and Analysis' which had taken over two years to prepare and was based on about five hundred documents specially written for the Conference. [48] Its title implies that it analyses why there are inequalities and injustices in land ownership. But the FAO is not in a position to analyse why. It is the representative of its member governments and to analyse why would be to direct an attack on many of them. To analyse what it has reviewed, the FAO would have had to explore why agrarian reform and rural development policies were designed and implemented in the way they were and why these policies were frequently ineffective in improving the productivity and livelihoods of most groups of rural poor. This would have involved investigating the special interests and social forces that determine development strategies for each country. It would also have had to cover the alliances between interest groups in the developed countries and the Third World. These issues are hardly raised in the document.

182. The FAO is still promoting technical solutions. There is much in the 'Review and Analysis' about modernisation of agriculture, as though this in itself will help the rural peasants forward. In fact, as has been argued, western style modernisation is likely to cut off peasant farmers from the two basic resources for production: land and water. Although there has already been much criticism of the Green Revolution mentality, even from within the UN, it was still very evident in the Conference literature.

183. Land reform and agrarian reform are presented both in the 'Review and Analysis' and in the 'Action Plan' as things which can be packaged and implemented with inputs from external aid and investment. It is certainly possible to impose land reform and rural development on people but the result is unlikely to be successful. Genuine reform has to include a shift of political power. It cannot be done to people; it has to be done *by* people.

184.   At the Preparatory Committee of WCARRD in March and at the Conference in July 1979, governments which have failed to provide elementary economic and social justice to their own people were the most strident in demanding access to international markets, improved terms of trade, transfer of resources and an increase in the flow of aid. This is an easy way to divert interest and concern from the real need for reform of power structures within countries.

185.   A significant lobby group went to the Rome Conference to question the official views that were being put forward there. They came from the developed and the developing countries and were all people who cared about the future of the poor of the world and who, in many cases, had worked beside them sharing their oppression and pain. Their role, they believed, was to publicise specific case studies relating to these people's struggles in order to highlight the inconsistencies of much that was being said in the Conference. An early version of this Oxfam report was part of their material. The group took a Declaration of their main concerns to Rome which is considered important enough to print in full. It was entitled 'The Rome Declaration on Agrarian Conflicts — False Premises/False Promises' and is reproduced at the end of this report as an appendix.

 **Conclusion**

186. The discussions and conclusions of the Agrarian Reform Conference make it clear that there has been little change in the thinking of international decision-makers. Nor do the much-heralded recommendations of the Independent Commission on International Development Issues, headed by Willy Brandt, give rise to any greater optimism. [49] The decision-makers will continue to give the kind of government-to-government and multilateral aid which reinforces the existing power structures which oppress poor people. As the authors of a recent study, 'Aid as Obstacle', so aptly say, "The basic fallacy inherent in official development assistance policy is that it can reach the powerless through the powerful." [50]

187. This report has been more about the problems and difficulties of land tenure systems than about solutions. That is right; it is not up to us to offer solutions to the people of the developing countries. What we in the rich countries should be trying to do is to remove some of the obstacles which prevent people from feeding themselves. Two obvious areas for investigation are international, multilateral aid and investment. Journalists and researchers both have a role here.

188. Anyone who still doubts whether this subject is important and who still does not believe that hunger is about politics and power and unequal wealth should consider how they would view the problem if they had been born into a landless peasant's family in Latin America or Asia.

APPENDIX

The Rome Declaration on Agrarian Conflict:

False Promises/False Premises Embodied in the World Conference on Agrarian Reform and Rural Development, Rome, July 12~20,1979

FALSE PREMISES

I. FUNCTION OF WCARRD

False premise: WCARRD reflects the growing appreciation by many governments of the need for agrarian reform. The conference was called, therefore, to assist governments to better understand the policies necessary to achieve rural development.

NO. Through WCARRD, many governments hope to divert attention from themselves as causes of rural suffering. They hope to lay the blame elsewhere – on obstinate local rural elites, on the scarcity of funds, on unavoidable conflicts in priorities, and on unfair international terms of trade. Moreover, many governments hope to make legitimate their promotion of modernisation, trade, foreign aid and transnational corporate investment even though such activities are already contributing to increased landlessness and hunger.

The function of this conference is to proclaim good intentions when, in many cases, the intentions are to protect vested interests; to proclaim progress where, in many places, there is greater suffering; to portray as friends of the poor not only those who are trying to promote their interests but also those actively involved in repressing them. If the intended function of this conference had been otherwise, non-governmental groups, including peasant-based organisations, would have been encouraged to share in shaping the conference. They have not been.

Only the rhetoric of agrarian reform has improved. But 'appropriate terminology' cannot hide the reality that for the majority of people, the concentration of control over the means to produce food is tightening. That WCARRD has been given so little weight by most governments itself indicates that for them agrarian reform is a dead issue.

II. REDISTRIBUTION

False premise: Control over productive assets – land, water, credit, access to markets – is only one of many problems. Parallel to it are other problems, such as rapid population growth, malnutrition, low production levels, and environmental degradation.

NO. Such a formulation obscures cause and effect. It is the distribution of control over productive assets that in large part determines the other factors. Only when people share democratically in control over resources can they create a context in which it is both rational and feasible to 1) choose to have fewer children 2) increase production and 3) protect their environment.

III. OBSTACLES TO REFORM

False premise: The primary obstacles to reforming control over productive assets are constitutional barriers, ambiguities in land reform legislation, the lack of funds, and the scarcity of land.

NO. The primary obstacle to reform is the power of the established dominant groups, often backed by considerable foreign resources (through such channels as the World Bank, FAO, transnational corporations, regional development banks and bilateral programmes). Such groups often employ the above tactics and rationalisation to further delay a just redistribution. Land scarcity, for example, is a false obstacle; one of the world's most land scarce countries has carried out one of the most successful land reforms (China). Land reform does not necessarily mean dividing up the land into little plots. The goal, rather, is a just and genuine sharing of control over the production process.

IV. THE ABSENCE OF CONFLICT

False premise: Agrarian reform and rural development are essentially conflict free. The only conflicts that emerge are those among several equally legitimate priorities competing for scarce resources.

NO. Agrarian reform cannot avoid the dismantling of power structures and therefore, social conflict. Such conflict **already** exists. In its most brutal and visible form those who benefit from the status quo fight tooth and nail any attempts at agrarian reform. Elites aggressively resist not only reform but even movements merely pressing for the implementation of existing legal provisions, such as minimum wage laws and the non-alienation of tribal lands. Violence and suffering become the daily reality for more and more of the world's people in countries like the Philippines, Nicaragua, Brazil and Chile to name just a few. Less visibly, we find growing daily violence against people in the form of malnutrition, joblessness and the diseases of poverty.

V. AGRARIAN REFORM,
A THIRD WORLD PROBLEM

False premise: Agrarian reform and rural development are Third World problems. Countries like the United States have solved their fundamental agrarian and agricultural problems and therefore represent a model to be followed by those less advanced.

NO. The root cause of hunger in the Third World — the tightening of economic, and therefore political, grip of a few — is intensifying in the industrial countries, particularly the United States. The destruction of agricultural resources, the growing impoverishment of farmers, rural landlessness and unemployment, the exploitation of over a million immigrant and migrant labourers, rising food prices, and unhealthy food additives — all associated with the tightening of control over the food system — are only a few of the costs.

Equally true, agricultural 'modernisation' à la the United States model means high production at very high risk. Deepening fossil fuel dependency, heavy doses of toxic chemicals, extreme geographic crop specialisation, the narrowing of genetic diversity, and the concentration of decision-making power in fewer and fewer industrial corporations, create a model of vulnerability, not a model of security.

Finally, agriculture à la the United States model means a heavy reliance on exports to maintain US farm income. Through massive 'food aid' and 'market development' strategies, people in other countries are made dependent on imports of questionable future availability and price stability.

FALSE PROMISES

VI. LAND REFORM

False promise: All land reforms reflect a desire by the government to help the rural poor. Governments and international agencies can carry out agrarian reform and rural development on behalf of the poor.

NO. Many so-called land reforms have been inspired and carried out by dominant groups to serve their own interests, not those of the rural poor. Such reforms have ignored those most in need — the many poor workers totally deprived of land. They have exempted those who put land into production for export. At best they have allowed tenants — often a pitifully small number — to buy land from their landlords, often under onerous terms. The net effect has been to strengthen the existing rural power structure, not dislodge it. Such pseudo reforms must never be confused with the redistribution of economic and political power carried out with the active participation of the rural dispossessed.

Genuine agrarian reform and rural development commence only once people struggle to create their own institutions, responsive to their needs. While recognizing the critical role to be played by leadership accountable to the people, it must be understood that agrarian reform cannot be done **to** people. Nor can it be done **for** people. The process of reform is as important as the reform itself.

VII. TARGETTING THE POOR

False promise: Where redistribution of control over productive resources is not politically feasible, rural development can occur anyway by targetting programmes toward the poorest groups.

NO. It is upon this hope that many lobby for 'better' aid projects. Without first confronting inequities in control, the benefits from technological innovations, agricultural extension programmes, credit, co-operatives, improvements in physical infrastructure and food-for-work programmes, etc, inevitably get skewed toward the better off and more powerful groups. The economic and political marginalisation of the majority, and therefore rural poverty is intensified, not alleviated.

A few show-case projects that seem to benefit a small number of poor do exist. But their cost is generally so great as to make them irreplaceable. They are tolerated by the dominant groups only as long as they remain isolated and thus not threatening to the status quo. Most importantly, through such projects the poor are not fundamentally empowered to protect their interests.

VIII. MODERNISATION

False promise: The problem is that agricultural modernisation has left behind the great majority of rural people, mired in traditional patterns of poverty. Rural development means drawing more and more rural people into the modern sector.

NO. Modernisation of agriculture implies simply the introduction of new methods and technologies. In the vast majority of countries the real purpose of the modernisation of agriculture is to drain wealth from rural workers. Rural development, however, means an improvement in the lives of the majority of rural people — better diet and housing, more satisfying work and security, enhanced feelings of personal worth and increased decision-making power over personal and community life. New methods and new technologies are appropriate if and only if they foster rural development so understood.

The modernisation of agriculture has not simply 'left behind' the majority: rather, it has actively impoverished them by excluding them still further from control over productive assets. Only when the foundation is laid for equitable control of resources will improved agricultural production translate into improved living conditions. Rural development starts with agrarian reform.

IX. TRADE

False promise: Increased trade is progress. The rural economies of the developing countries need to be linked with the world economic system through trade.

NO. Trade structured to drain wealth has been a prime mechanism in under-developing the now poor countries. More of the same is not the answer.

Trade is promoted uncritically by elites whose control over productive resources allows them to profit by foreign sales at the expense of the majority. For them, export expansion is the way to compensate for the stagnating local market they helped to impoverish. Export profits are an incentive to further tighten their grip on resources as well as a means by which to do so.

Trade **can** be beneficial but only once basic needs are met locally and the income generated is controlled for the benefit of the entire society.

X. FOREIGN AID

False promise: Foreign assistance and transnational corporate investment are essential to rural development.

NO. Much of official foreign assistance and virtually all transnational corporate investment serve to reinforce the interests of only the minority who monopolise the productive resources. Re-distribution of control over those resources must come first. Then both aid and foreign corporations must be carefully evaluated for their potential to contribute to self-determined and equitable development.

XI. WOMEN AND DEVELOPMENT

False promise: Women must be increasingly incorporated into the development process.

NO. The issue is not one of bringing women into the economic process but of recognising and building upon the *de facto* contributions to the economic process. A development strategy that does not confront fundamental structural inequalities is likely to exacerbate the powerlessness of women. Wage relations and the de-mands of commercialisation can deprive women of the power they had exerted in traditional modes of production. Western-based development programmes have encouraged education, technical training, and credit to be directed almost exclusively toward males.

XII. PEOPLE'S PARTICIPATION

False promise: Governments and development agencies have come increasingly to see the need for 'people's participation' in development.

NO. Genuine participation of people in taking hold of development problems is what is being resisted, in many cases outlawed, in the very countries claiming to be for 'participation'. Where the hungry and landless organise to demand their rights they are often brutally repressed. The language of 'participation' is then used by governments to draw attention away from the suppression of their people's right to organise. Many decision-making policies now in vogue among governments, rather than being a tool for people's participation, extend and rationalise an elite-based government's control over the people.

People can be made to 'participate' in virtually any kind of project. The issue therefore is not so much who participates but who controls. To ensure genuine rural development, moreover, rural people must not merely control their own development programmes but participate in wielding national political and economic power to protect their interests.

Rome, July 12, 1979   The Rome Declaration Group

References

Those readers wishing to see any of the project files referred to in this paper should apply to the Overseas Director, Oxfam, 274 Banbury Road, Oxford OX2 7DZ, England.

1 Peter Stalker, "Growing Inequality". *New Internationalist,* No. 81, November 1979, p.5.

2 "Land Reform That Flopped". *The Guardian,* April 11, 1980.

3 FAO, *Review and Analysis of Agrarian Reform and Rural Development in the Developing Countries since the Mid-1960s.* Rome, December 1978, p.1.

4 Roger Plant, *Guatemala: Unnatural Disaster.* Latin America Bureau, London, 1978, p.80.

5 UNDP, *Rural Women's Participation in Development.* Geneva, 1980.

6 Oxfam Project – Haiti 43.

7 Susan George, *How the Other Half Dies: the Real Reasons for World Hunger.* Pelican Books, London, 1976.

   Susan George, *Feeding the Few: Corporate Control of Food.* Institute of Policy Studies, Washington and Amsterdam, 1979.

8 Correspondence with Field Staff in Latin America.

9 Tour Report from Oxfam Press Officer.

10 Oxfam Project – Bolivia 35.

11 Oxfam Project – Bolivia 39.

12 Oxfam Projects – Madhya Pradesh.

13 Oxfam Project – Bangladesh 84.

14 Oxfam Projects – Maharashtra.

15 Oxfam Project – Andhra Pradesh 22.

16 Oxfam Project – Andhra Pradesh 24s.

17 Personal communication.

18 R.C. Riddell, *The Land Problem in Rhodesia.* Mambo Press/CIIR, London, 1978, p.33.

19 R.C. Riddell, *The Land Question.* "From Rhodesia to Zimbabwe", No. 2, CIIR, London, p.38.

20 Susan George, *How the Other Half Dies.* op. cit.

21 Frances Moore Lappé and Joseph Collins, *Food First: Beyond the Myth of Scarcity.* Houghton Mifflin, Boston, 1977, pp.145-146.

22 "The Harrying of the Harijans". *The Guardian,* April 1980.

23 Robert Chambers, Seminar on Land Reform. ODI, London, 1979.

24 Reports from Oxfam Field Staff in Latin America.

25 Sartaj Aziz, *Rural Development: Learning From China.* Macmillan, London, 1978, p. xix.

26 World Council of Churches, *Report on the Situation of Human Rights in the Republic of Korea.* Geneva, May 1979.

27 "Land Reform that Flopped". *The Guardian,* op. cit.

28 Nitish De, *Adaptation of Traditional Systems of Agriculture in a Developing Economy.* National Labour Institute, New Delhi, 1977, p.3.

29 Pran Chopra, "The Plan Plants a Time Bomb". *Medico Friend Circle Bulletin,* No. 41, May 1979, Wardha, India, p.7.

30 For a discussion of the Gramdan Movement see Devi Prasad, *Gramdan: the Land Revolution of India.* War Resisters' International, London, undated.

31 "Political Strings on Foreign Aid Tightened". *The Guardian,* February 21, 1980.

32 Robert McNamara, *Address to the Board of Governors of the World Bank.* Nairobi, Kenya, September 24, 1973, p.10.

33 Ibid., p.18.

34 Annual Report from Oxfam Field Director in Brazil, 1979.

35 Oxfam Field Director's Report from Gujarat.

36 "Do Multinationals Really Create Jobs in the Third World?" *Wall Street Journal,* September 25, 1979.

37 Anthony Hall, *Drought and Irrigation in North-east Brazil.* Cambridge University Press, 1978.

38 World Bank, *Annual Report 1975.* Washington D.C.

39 Bernard Wideman, "Philippine Mountain People Declare War on Chico Dam Project". *AMPO,* Vol. 10, No. 3, 1978, pp. 24-29; and personal communication.

40 Betsy Hartman and James Boyce, *Bangladesh: Aid to the Needy.* Centre for International Policy, Washington D.C., May 1978.

41 Personal communication.

42 Susan George, *How the Other Half Dies.* op. cit.

43 B. Dasgupta, *Agrarian Change and the New Technology in India.* UNRISD Green Revolution Series, Geneva, 1977.

44 Keith Griffin, *The Political Economy of Agrarian Change: an Essay on the Green Revolution.* Macmillan, London, 1974, p.2.

45 Alan Riding, "US Food Aid seen Hurting Guatemala". *New York Times,* November 6, 1977.

46 Reports from an Oxfam-America researcher.
European Commission, *Food Aid.* Document 448:541232, Brussells, April 25, 1978.

47 Correspondence between UNRISD and WCARRD Secretariat.

48 FAO, *Review and Analysis . . . . .* op. cit.

49 *North-South: A Programme for Survival. Report of the Independent Com-*

mission on International Development Issues. Pan Books, London, 1980.
50 Frances Moore Lappé, Joseph Collins and David Kinley, *Aid as Obstacle: Twenty Questions About Our Foreign Aid and the Hungry.* Institute for Food and Development Policy, San Francisco, 1980.